Follow That Food Chain

A Temperate Forest Food Chain

A WHO-EATS-WHAT Adventure in North America

Rebecca Hogue Wojahn Donald Wojahn

Lerner Publications Company
Minneapolis

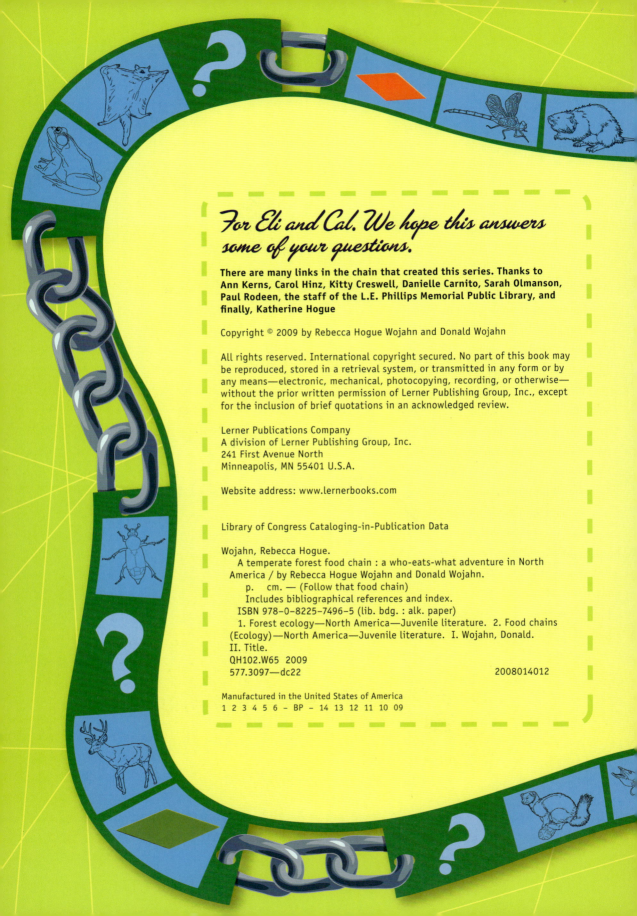

For Eli and Cal. We hope this answers some of your questions.

There are many links in the chain that created this series. Thanks to Ann Kerns, Carol Hinz, Kitty Creswell, Danielle Carnito, Sarah Olmanson, Paul Rodeen, the staff of the L.E. Phillips Memorial Public Library, and finally, Katherine Hogue

Lerner Publications Company
A division of Lerner Publishing Group, Inc.
241 First Avenue North
Minneapolis, MN 55401 U.S.A.

Website address: www.lernerbooks.com

Library of Congress Cataloging-in-Publication Data

Wojahn, Rebecca Hogue.
    A temperate forest food chain : a who-eats-what adventure in North
America / by Rebecca Hogue Wojahn and Donald Wojahn.
        p.   cm. — (Follow that food chain)
    Includes bibliographical references and index.
    ISBN 978-0-8225-7496-5 (lib. bdg. : alk. paper)
    1. Forest ecology—North America—Juvenile literature. 2. Food chains
(Ecology)—North America—Juvenile literature. I. Wojahn, Donald.
II. Title.
QH102.W65 2009
577.3097—dc22   2008014012

Manufactured in the United States of America
1 2 3 4 5 6 – BP – 14 13 12 11 10 09

Contents

WELCOME TO THE WOODS . . . 4

CHOOSE A TERTIARY CONSUMER . . . 6

PLANTS AND TREES . . . 24

A FOREST FOOD WEB . . . 44

GLOSSARY . . . 60

FURTHER READING AND WEBSITES . . . 61

SELECTED BIBLIOGRAPHY . . . 62

INDEX . . . 63

Introduction
WELCOME TO THE WOODS

Step into the woods on a warm summer morning. See how the light dims? Feel how the air cools? Sunlight filters through the branches of the trees overhead. Some trees are as tall as nine-story buildings. Others are just small saplings starting to grow. Bushes and shrubs crowd between the trees and tug at your shoulders. Plants cling to your legs and ankles, while your shoes sink into the mosses and dead leaves covering the ground.

The forest is alive with sound. Insects buzz, birds call, squirrels chatter, and—what was that? There's a bear crashing through the brush, just up ahead!

Deep woods such as these used to sprawl across the northeastern part of North America. But as new settlers spread across the continent, they cut down the forests. They used the timber for homes and firewood, and turned the land into farms. Many woods have disappeared forever, but some remain. And some have grown back. Inside these forest **habitats** live thousands of **species** of animals. Come meet a few of them here in this book.

A Temperate Forest

Temperate describes a climate that does not have extreme temperatures. A temperate climate also has a change of seasons and moderate amounts of rain, snow, and dry weather.

Choose a
TERTIARY CONSUMER

All the living things in the forest are necessary for its health and survival. From the moss under your shoes to the black bear lurking up ahead, the living things are all connected. Animals and other organisms feed on and transfer energy to one another. This is called a **food chain** or a **food web**.

In food chains, the strongest **predators** are called **tertiary consumers**. They hunt other animals for food and have few natural enemies. Some of the animals they eat are called **secondary consumers**. Secondary consumers are also predators. They hunt plant-eating animals. Plant eaters are **primary consumers**.

Plants are **producers**. Using energy from the sun, they produce their own food. Plants take in **nutrients** from the soil. They also provide nutrients to the animals that eat them.

Decomposers are insects or **bacteria** that break down dead plants and animals. Decomposers change them into the nutrients found in the soil.

The plants and animals in a food chain depend on each other. Sometimes there's a break in the chain, such as one type of animal dying out. This loss ripples through the rest of the habitat.

Begin your journey through the temperate forest food web by choosing a tertiary consumer. These large **carnivores**, or meat eaters, are at the top of the food chain. That means, for the most part, they don't have any enemies in the woods (except for humans).

When it's time for the tertiary consumer to eat, pick its meal and flip to that page. As you go through the book, don't be surprised if you backtrack and end up where you never expected to be. That's how food webs work—they're complicated. And watch out for those dead ends! When you hit one of those, you have to go back to page 7 and start over with another tertiary consumer.

The main role an animal plays in the forest food web is identified by a color-coded shape. Here is the key to that code:

TERTIARY CONSUMER

PRODUCER

SECONDARY CONSUMER

PRIMARY CONSUMER

DECOMPOSER

To choose . . .

. . . an American black bear, TURN TO PAGE 8.

. . . a gray wolf, TURN TO PAGE 28.

. . . a great horned owl, TURN TO PAGE 20.

. . . a Canada lynx, TURN TO PAGE 27.

. . . a bald eagle, TURN TO PAGE 38.

To learn more about a forest food web, GO TO PAGE 44.

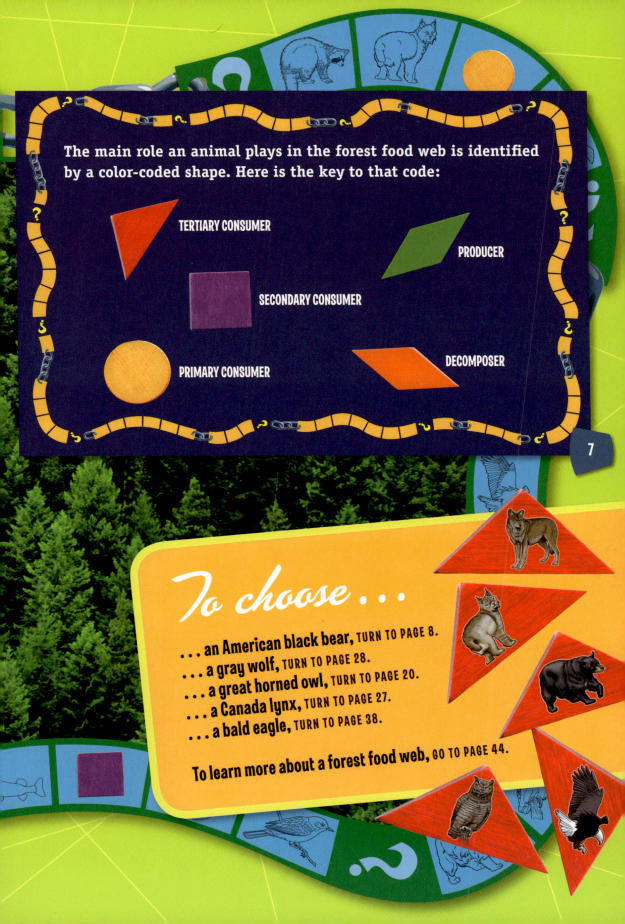

AMERICAN BLACK BEAR (*Ursus americanus*)

The American black bear stands on her hind legs to sniff the spring air. She has an excellent sense of smell. She smells the garbage dump down the road, a campsite with roasting marshmallows a few miles away, and a rotting deer carcass in the woods. So many delicious aromas!

She is almost always hungry. All winter the bear hibernated. She was in a resting state all day, every day. She went six months without eating or going to the bathroom. And now she weighs only half of what she did last fall.

Her two cubs wrestle with each other in the leaves nearby. They were born in hibernation. The three of them left their home, called a den, when the cubs were about three months old. The cubs weigh about 8 pounds (3.6 kilograms)—the size of a newborn human baby.

The mother bear's ears prick up and then flatten back. Another bear—a male one—has wandered into her meadow! And baby bears are sometimes just the kind of snack for male bears. The mother bear huffs and clicks her teeth at the male in a warning.

But the male bear ignores her. He heads straight for the tumbling cubs.

The mother bear starts to run. Her cubs see her. And they know the routine. They scramble up a nearby tree as fast as they can.

Black bear cubs get ready to climb a tree.

The mother bear scares off the male bear. Then she stands on her hind legs and—*scraaatch*. She drags her sharp claws through the bark in a tree. There. That will serve as a sign to other bears that this is her territory. The bear will do anything to protect her cubs and provide the food they need to survive.

The three of them wander on, always looking for food. A road stretches ahead. The bear sniffs at the edge. Suddenly, a huge logging truck blasts over the top of the hill. It is so loud and moving so fast, she is not sure what to do. It's coming right at her.

At the last second, the truck swerves around her, blaring its horn. She's lucky. So are her cubs. They need her protection for another whole year. They can't survive without her.

Bear Facts

Black bears aren't always black. Some are brown, blond, honey, cinnamon, white, and blue (a dark, bluish gray color). Adults weigh from 125 to 600 pounds (57 to 272 kg). Adult males can grow to be 6 feet (2 meters) long. For their size, they are very fast. Adults can reach a top speed of 30 miles (48 kilometers) per hour.

With a deep roar and five long claws on each paw, a bear seems fierce. But they are shy animals and like to be alone. In fact, their main enemy is people. Most bears don't reach their natural life span of twenty-one to thirty-three years because of humans. Some bears are killed by hunters. Some are killed in road accidents or in other run-ins with humans. Even though people are their biggest danger, black bears only attack humans when startled or when their food or babies are threatened.

The cubs also must gain enough weight by autumn to live through another winter in hibernation. And their mother must too. For all three, that means eating—anything and everything. Bears are **omnivores**—they eat both meat and plants. Eighty-five percent of their diet comes from forest plants, berries, nuts, and seeds. Bears also eat carrion—the bodies of animals that have died or were killed by other predators. And they like to snack on small rodents—lots of them.

Last night for dinner, the bears stuffed themselves with . . .

This black bear holds the dinner he just caught—a salmon.

. . . a northern pike scooped out of the shallows of a lake. To see what another northern pike is up to, TURN TO PAGE 58.

. . . a young white-tailed deer. To see what another white-tailed deer is up to, TURN TO PAGE 46.

. . . a northern flying squirrel. To see what another northern flying squirrel is up to, TURN TO PAGE 19.

. . . an elk grazing along the edge of the meadow. To see what another elk is up to, TURN TO PAGE 14.

. . . plants and berries. To read about the plants and berries of the woods, TURN TO PAGE 24.

MUSKRAT

(Ondatra zibethicus)

The shiny brown **mammal** slips into the water from the bank without a splash. No, it's not a beaver. This is a muskrat, swimming silently through the weeds in the shallows of the lake. Her tail is long, scaly, and black, with no fur. But, unlike a beaver's tail, it is thin like a rat's. Her hind feet are partially webbed, making her swimming seem almost effortless.

A shadow passes overhead. It could be a predator. The muskrat dives down. She can hide underwater for up to fifteen minutes— long enough for the danger to pass.

Underwater, she glides through the thick weeds. Not far from here, she's made a mound-shaped house called a lodge. Muskrats make their lodges from uprooted weeds and mud. The lodge entrance is underwater. Everything she needs is close to her lodge. She seldom goes very far from home. But she's always busy rebuilding—and looking for food. *Last night for dinner, she munched on . . .*

Muskrat Problems

As with many of the animals in the woods, humans are the muskrats' biggest enemy. Muskrats dig paths through the weeds in the shallow waters, and they often burrow into the banks of lakes and rivers. Sometimes these burrows cause the shore to sink or collapse. This causes problems for human structures, such as bridges and retaining walls. Because of this, people often shoot or trap muskrats. Most muskrats only live for one year.

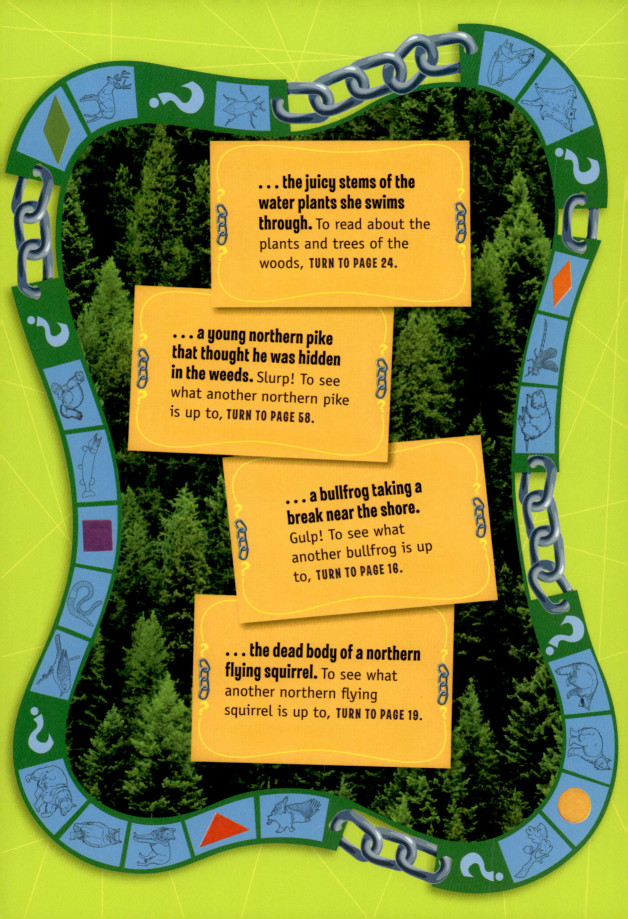

. . . **the juicy stems of the water plants she swims through.** To read about the plants and trees of the woods, TURN TO PAGE 24.

. . . **a young northern pike that thought he was hidden in the weeds.** Slurp! To see what another northern pike is up to, TURN TO PAGE 58.

. . . **a bullfrog taking a break near the shore.** Gulp! To see what another bullfrog is up to, TURN TO PAGE 16.

. . . **the dead body of a northern flying squirrel.** To see what another northern flying squirrel is up to, TURN TO PAGE 19.

ELK *(Cervus elaphus)*

You've hit a **DEAD END!** These supersized deer with shaggy manes wandered most of the United States and Canada for hundreds of years. Now they are found only in small areas.

Elk have beautiful antlers—and they use them too! In September, when the antlers are fully grown, their length can be 4 to 5 feet (1 to 1.5 meters) across. Males will often battle and stab one another with their antlers over female elk. But it was not their own fighting that made elk almost disappear from the woods. It was hunting and timber logging.

Ivory Teeth

Elk are the only North American animals to have ivory teeth. Ivory is the hard, white material that elephant tusks are also made of. Elk have two ivory teeth—their upper front ones. Historically, hunters prized these teeth. Native Americans often use them for decoration. An organization called the Benevolent and Protective Order of the Elks used elk teeth as a symbol for their group.

KIRTLAND'S WARBLER

(Dendroica kirtlandii)

Sorry, that predator's stomach is going to have to go on grumbling. Kirtland's warblers (also called jack pine warblers) are endangered and a **DEAD END**.

Kirtland's warblers love to nest in the bottom branches of jack pine forests in the northern United States. But now jack pine forests are becoming harder to find. Oddly enough, human protection of the forest has caused some of this bird's trouble. The jack pines' pinecones open up and release their seeds only in intense heat, such as that of a forest fire. Not all forest fires are accidents caused by humans. Some naturally happen due to hot, dry conditions or lightning strikes. And these fires are an important cycle in the forest. If people try to stop all forest fires, even natural ones, the jack pines' seeds never fall to the ground and take root. When this happens, the Kirtland's warblers have fewer places to build their nests.

This jack pine forest is being regrown as a habitat for the Kirtland's warbler.

Parasite Birds

Kirtland's warblers have an invader to worry about: cowbirds. In the past, cowbirds and Kirtland's warblers each had a separate habitat. They were pushed together into the same habitat when the forests were cleared for logging. Cowbirds are parasites. They lay their eggs in other birds' nests. The two sets of chicks are hatched together, and the warbler mother feeds them all. But the cowbird chicks are so pushy that they eat all the food. The warbler chicks often starve or are pushed right out of the nest.

BULLFROG (*Rana catesbeiana* Shaw)

With a stretch of his legs, the bullfrog bounds 6 feet (2 meters) down the shore of the lake. He spends his whole life near the water. He's carefully marked out his territory here. And with his size—his body alone is as long as your foot!—he's not afraid to throw his weight around. If another male enters his area, he will push, shove, and grab the invader until he backs off.

16

The bullfrog wasn't always this big, though. Bullfrog tadpoles take two years to develop. He spent his first winter swimming under the ice. That's why bullfrogs aren't found in swampy areas, as other frogs are. Bullfrogs need deeper water to survive.

Tadpoles have no way to fight off predators. All they can do is hide. Young bullfrogs, newly out of the tadpole stage, also try to avoid predators. When you walk in the woods, you can hear them jump in the water to escape from you!

Flatworms

In 1995 Minnesota schoolchildren on a field trip found something that alarmed scientists. Nearly half the frogs the students caught had extra or missing legs. Since then many other people around the United States and Canada have found frogs with limb problems, and scientists have been working hard to figure out why. They believe that many of these deformities are because of a flatworm parasite, a microscopic worm that burrows inside a tadpole egg. But this flatworm has been around for a long time. Why would it suddenly cause so many problems? Scientists worry that it might be because of some other small change in the habitat or food chain that we don't even understand yet.

Adult bullfrogs are quick, alert hunters. They have strong tongues. A bullfrog's tongue twists and flips its **prey** so that the prey is crushed against the teeth on the top of the bullfrog's mouth. And what goes in that mouth? Bullfrogs eat pretty much anything they can stretch their mouth around! *Last night for dinner, this bullfrog gulped . . .*

This bullfrog caught a dragonfly.

. . . **a Hine's emerald dragonfly nymph.** To see what another Hine's emerald dragonfly is up to, TURN TO PAGE 23.

. . . **young northern pikes swimming by.** To see what another northern pike is up to, TURN TO PAGE 58.

. . . **a young northern short-tailed shrew wandering too close.** To see what another northern short-tailed shrew is up to, TURN TO PAGE 54.

. . . **a northern ringneck snake that thought he was hidden under a log.** To see what another northern ringneck snake is up to, TURN TO PAGE 42.

. . . **a cloud of insects buzzing on top of the water.** To read about other insects of the woods, TURN TO PAGE 36.

NORTHERN FLYING SQUIRREL
(Glaucomys sabrinus)

The northern flying squirrel darts around the top of an oak tree. He's survived the winter in a hollow in the trunk. It's been crowded. Nine squirrels were jammed in a space a little bigger than a shoebox. (And you thought it was hard to share the bathroom with your brother or sister!) But the body heat from all those squirrels kept the nest warm. It stayed cozy, even when the snow stacked up and the wind blew so hard that the tree bent and swayed.

19

The squirrel scampers to the end of a branch and—jumps! As he falls through the air, he stretches his legs out wide. A loose fold of skin between his front and back legs, called the patagium, catches the air. He glides like a paper airplane on his way down. His whole body, from his paws to his tail, is made for these flights. Sometimes he can soar as far as 60 feet (18 meters)!

Of course, there are dangers too. Last year he glided into a barbed wire fence and snagged his patagium. He barely survived. But today he makes it safely to the forest floor and starts looking again for more food. Can you guess what he ate last night for dinner?

Nuts and acorns hidden in the leaves on the ground? Or seeds and berries that are just coming out on the trees?

To read about the plants and trees of the woods, **TURN TO PAGE 24.**

GREAT HORNED OWL *(Bubo virginianus)*

The great horned owl perches silently in the upper branches of the maple tree. Unlike other birds that soar in search of **prey**, the owl is happy to watch and wait. Owls will hunt just about anything that moves below. They are one of the few animals to brave skunks and porcupines. Sometimes owl behavior causes problems with the animals that are rare in the woods. Owls don't know about endangered species. They will hunt animals on the verge of becoming **extinct**, such as ospreys or peregrine falcons.

As the owl roosts, a crow flaps by and perches above her. He caws loudly. The call soon brings other crows. They fill the branches around the owl and begin screeching at her. The racket grows louder and louder with each crow that appears. It's not long before one crow breaks off from the group. It dives straight at the owl's head!

At the last second, the crow pulls up and rejoins the crowd. The owl fluffs her feathers, unruffled by the crow. She could easily kill it, if she wanted to. In fact, owls are crows' main enemy. That is exactly why the crows are pestering, or "mobbing," the owl. They want to drive her off. The mob continues to grow bigger and louder, and the owl flies off after a few more minutes.

Noisy Owls

Think you know what an owl sounds like? That "hoo-hoo" hooting is just one of the sounds that comes from great horned owls. While both males and females hoot, males' calls are much deeper. Owls also snap their beaks, make a "me-ow"-like noise, coo, and "bark." When they are threatened or disturbed, they might shriek or growl or call out a loud, "whaaa whaaaaaa-a-a-aarrk." Owls are noisiest in the early evenings. Their hoots can be heard for miles at night.

She heads back to her lair. Owls don't build their own nests. They use the nests of other birds or animals. Below her nest, the forest floor is littered with hard wads of bone and hair. These are owl pellets. Owls spit up bits of food—mostly bones, hair, and feathers—that they can't digest. People dissect these pellets to learn more about owls. Sometimes whole skeletons of small birds or rodents can be found inside them and pieced back together.

Last night's pellets are there below. They show that last night she snatched . . .

This owl is roosting in a stick nest.

. . . **a northern pike swimming near the surface of the lake.** To see what another northern pike is up to, TURN TO PAGE 58.

. . . **a Kirtland's warbler roosting under a jack pine.** To see what another Kirtland's warbler is up to, TURN TO PAGE 15.

. . . **a northern short-tailed shrew shuffling through the underbrush.** To see what another northern short-tailed shrew is up to, TURN TO PAGE 54.

. . . **a bullfrog croaking near shore.** To see what another bullfrog is up to, TURN TO PAGE 16.

. . . **a young pine marten darting after a squirrel.** To see what another pine marten is up to, TURN TO PAGE 56.

. . . **a northern ringneck snake that peeked out from under his log a little too long.** To see what another northern ringneck snake is up to, TURN TO PAGE 42.

. . . **a baby raccoon left alone by its mother.** To see what another raccoon is up to, TURN TO PAGE 50.

. . . **a muskrat chewing some lake weeds.** To see what another muskrat is up to, TURN TO PAGE 12.

HINE'S EMERALD DRAGONFLY

(Somatochlora hineana)

The dragonfly stretches his wings wide in the sun. He has just crawled out of the shallow marsh water and from his **larva** shell. His wings are too wet to fly. He is extremely at risk to predators right now. Although other dragonflies flit around, he is the only Hine's emerald dragonfly here today. His species has been endangered since 1995. If he can't find a mate, there'll be even fewer of them.

Creatures looking to munch on Hine's emerald dragonflies have reached a **DEAD END**. There just aren't enough left for a meal.

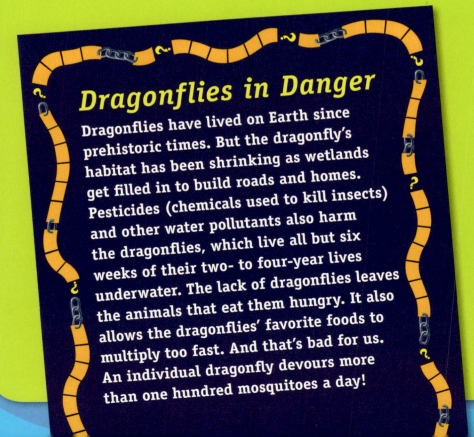

Dragonflies in Danger

Dragonflies have lived on Earth since prehistoric times. But the dragonfly's habitat has been shrinking as wetlands get filled in to build roads and homes. Pesticides (chemicals used to kill insects) and other water pollutants also harm the dragonflies, which live all but six weeks of their two- to four-year lives underwater. The lack of dragonflies leaves the animals that eat them hungry. It also allows the dragonflies' favorite foods to multiply too fast. And that's bad for us. An individual dragonfly devours more than one hundred mosquitoes a day!

PLANTS AND TREES

Trees may be the first plants we notice in the forest. But no one plant can represent all the plants of the woods. There are so many species of plants, and they all have such different jobs. Each provides for different animals in the forest.

Scientists often divide the forest into five layers of producers. The highest layer is made up of trees 60 to 100 feet (18 to 30 meters) tall. Oaks, ash, pines, maple, and birch tower over the other plants. Their branches and leaves interlace high overhead, forming a **canopy**. The canopy provides shade and shelter to the animals and soil below.

Below the canopy are smaller trees and saplings. Someday they will stretch high enough to be at the top. But canopies take time to grow. When a forest is cut down, there is no shortcut to regrowing it. The only way is to wait, sometimes hundreds of years.

A bigleaf maple tree and an alder tree form a canopy in the forest.

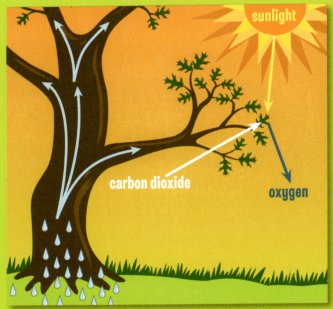

sunlight

carbon dioxide

oxygen

Plants make food and oxygen through photosynthesis. Plants draw in carbon dioxide (a gas found in air) and water. Then they use the energy from sunlight to turn the carbon dioxide and water into their food.

Under the saplings are the shrubs, and below them are the herb layer. At these two lower levels, many of the forest animals find food from leaves, seeds, or berries. The lowest layer is the ground layer. Here's where you'll find the mosses and lichens (plant-like living things).

All of these plants are necessary for the survival of the woods, and all of these plants need the same three things to survive: water, sunlight, and nutrients from the soil. *Last night for dinner, these plants, from the mighty white pine to the scaly lichen on the stone, soaked up the nutrients in the soil that were left behind from . . .*

Mushrooms grow on a decaying log on the ground layer.

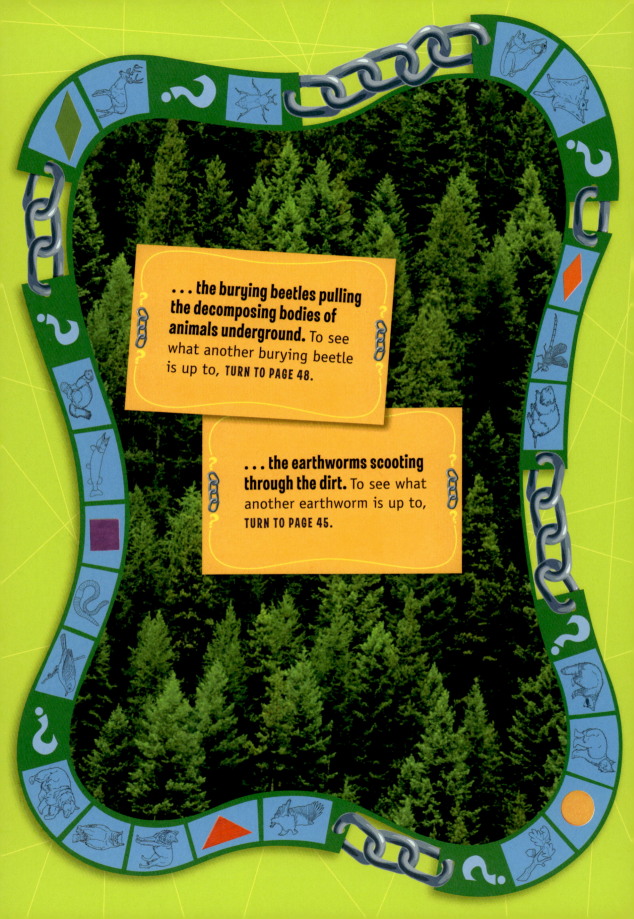

. . . the burying beetles pulling the decomposing bodies of animals underground. To see what another burying beetle is up to, TURN TO PAGE 48.

. . . the earthworms scooting through the dirt. To see what another earthworm is up to, TURN TO PAGE 45.

CANADA LYNX *(Lynx canadensis)*

Uh-oh. You didn't make it very far! This is a **DEAD END**. Canada lynx are listed as a threatened species. That means they are likely to be endangered in the near future. They have become so rare that scientists are not even sure how many are left in the wild.

Tertiary consumers such as the Canada lynx are much more likely to find themselves threatened or endangered than animals lower on the food chain. They are predators. Historically people have been afraid of them and killed them off. Also, they usually need much more space to live and hunt. They are more likely to have people crowd their territory—as when new houses are built on the edge of the wilderness. And finally, if any animals lower on the food chain are struggling to survive, that means there are fewer of them for these predators to eat. So eventually, the predators' numbers drop too.

In the case of the Canada lynx, it's the lack of habitat for the snowshoe hare—their main food—that has them in trouble. As the snowshoe hares become harder to find, Canada lynx have all but disappeared.

GRAY WOLF *(Canis lupus)*

The gray wolf trots along through the brush. His pack of seven follows closely behind. They each have a job in the pack. This wolf's job is to lead. He picks the trails. He eats first. He makes the decisions for the pack. He is the pack's alpha male. The rest of the wolves will do what he wants.

The pack hunts for food. However, they won't roam far. This pack is sticking to one place until their pups grow big enough to join the hunt—usually in late summer. During the fall and winter months, the pack moves more widely. Wolves hunt over more space than any other land **mammals**, except humans. They can rove from 10 to 1,000 square miles (26 to 2,600 square kilometers)!

The alpha male stops to sniff. He bristles. He's caught a whiff of another wolf. His pack's territory has been carefully marked out with urine to keep other packs away. The pack picks up its pace, eager to find the invader. They burst out into a clearing. There stands the intruding wolf.

A gray wolf submits to the alpha male of his pack.

The wolves in the pack bare their teeth, ready to fight. But this is a lone wolf. He knows he's much more likely to survive with a pack. He tucks his tail between his legs. He crouches low and sniffs the leader's face. The pack leader holds his head and tail high. He pricks up his ears and, with that, lets the lone wolf join their pack's hunt.

There used to be a lot more gray wolves in these woods. But when the bison, elk, and moose disappeared, the wolves had to find other food. They turned to people's livestock, stealing chickens and sheep from nearby farms. People tried to keep the wolves away by poisoning, trapping, and hunting them. Until the 1960s, rewards were offered for killing gray wolves. People would get paid for every wolf hide they brought in. By 1974 gray wolves were in danger of becoming extinct.

This pack passes by a cabin in the woods now. Two dogs are chained in the yard. The pack growls and approaches. Then— BANG—a gunshot rings out.

The pack scatters and runs. They are lucky—no one is hurt. They all join up again a few miles away.

Laws have been passed to protect the gray wolf so it doesn't become extinct. Wildlife experts are reintroducing, or bringing back, the gray wolf into certain wilderness areas. They hope this will increase the number of wolves in the wild. It's working. In fact, gray wolves are doing so well in some places that the U.S. government has taken them off the **endangered species list**.

A pack of gray wolves walks through a meadow.

But that doesn't keep them safe from everyday dangers—such as getting shot. Many people still misunderstand wolves. While it is true that wolves may attack dogs or livestock, they are much more likely to hunt sick or injured deer or other animals. In fact, they help weed out the weaker animals. And there has never been a case where a human has died of a wolf attack. Still, biologists are waiting to see what will happen with wolves living closer than ever to humans.

For today it looks as if this wolf pack will go hungry. Last night, however, was a different story. **Last night for dinner, the pack tracked down . . .**

Hungry Like a Wolf

Wolves can go up to two weeks without eating. They need about 4 pounds (2 kilograms) of food a day to survive. But they don't usually eat every day. Wolves know that some days there might not be anything to eat, so they stuff themselves when they do kill something. Wolves have been known to eat up to 22 pounds (10 kg) in one feeding. That's almost one-third of their weight! Can you imagine eating eighty-eight quarter-pound hamburgers in one sitting?

. . . a pine marten caught scampering across the pine needles. To see what another pine marten is up to, TURN TO PAGE 56.

. . . a northern flying squirrel that surprised the pack as he glided to the ground. To see what another northern flying squirrel is up to, TURN TO PAGE 19.

. . . a raccoon rubbing his food in a river. To see what another raccoon is up to, TURN TO PAGE 50.

. . . an elk that's been sick all winter. To see what another elk is up to, TURN TO PAGE 14.

. . . a panicked white-tailed deer that gave a good chase. To see what another white-tailed deer is up to, TURN TO PAGE 46.

. . . an American beaver distracted by the fall of a large tree. To see what another American beaver is up to, TURN TO PAGE 34.

. . . burying beetles on their way to a new carcass. To see what another pair of burying beetles are up to, TURN TO PAGE 48.

DEER TICK *(Ixodes scapularis)*

The deer tick clings to the tip of the long grass, waiting for an animal to pass. She's found her way to this deer path by smell and by sensing the body heat of the passing **mammals**. Even though this creature is definitely a creepy-crawly, it's not a bug. Ticks are actually arachnids—in the same family as spiders.

Ticks have four stages of life—egg, **larva**, **nymph**, and adult. This tick is a nymph—almost an adult. She's hunting for any animal to bite. When she first grabs onto an animal, her saliva numbs the spot so the animal doesn't know it's been bitten. She'll fill herself on the animal's blood until she's full. Then she drops off. In the autumn, she'll shed her skin and molt into an adult.

A tick has three different hosts (creatures it lives off of) in its lifetime. It has one host as a larva, one as a nymph, and one as an adult. After feasting on her host, an adult female will lay eggs—four thousand of them—in the dirt. And, if at any time she can't find a host, she can survive up to two years without eating!

For the last few nights, this tick has been slurping the blood of . . .

Disease Carriers

Deer ticks will feed off a surprising number of animals. Because they feed off multiple hosts, they carry diseases from one animal to another. Ticks can carry the bacteria or parasites that cause Lyme disease, human anaplasmosis, babesiosis, and Rocky Mountain spotted fever. These diseases can make animals and people very sick.

. . . a northern short-tailed shrew. To see what another northern short-tailed shrew is up to, TURN TO PAGE 54.

. . . a pine marten. To see what another pine marten is up to, TURN TO PAGE 56.

. . . a Canada lynx. To see what another Canada lynx is up to, TURN TO PAGE 27.

. . . a northern flying squirrel. To see what another northern flying squirrel is up to, TURN TO PAGE 19.

. . . a gray wolf. To see what another gray wolf is up to, TURN TO PAGE 28.

. . . an elk. To see what another elk is up to, TURN TO PAGE 14.

. . . a black bear. To see what another black bear is up to, TURN TO PAGE 8.

. . . an American beaver. To see what another American beaver is up to, TURN TO PAGE 34.

AMERICAN BEAVER *(Castor canadensis)*

Crash! A willow tree slams to the ground. The beaver has gnawed through 5 inches (13 centimeters) of tree in less than five minutes—faster than it probably took you to eat your breakfast this morning! He pauses to check again to see if any predators are about. Things are still quiet, so he begins the work of trimming the branches off the fallen tree. Then he drags the branches to the edge of the creek.

Beavers' lives depend on trees. Beavers use trees for food and to build their homes. The beavers can't drag the branches very well on land. But once in the water, the beaver can tow the branch while swimming. He tows it back to his home, called a lodge. There he'll either add it to his home or submerge it in the water for a mid-winter snack later on.

The beaver's lodge is a pile of branches wedged across the creek. It's hollow underneath, and this is where the beaver lives. The largest beaver lodges can be 6 to 8 feet (2 to 2.4 meters) high and one-quarter of a mile (0.4 kilometer) long! This beaver's home is only a few feet high. But it's big enough that it has dammed up the creek and created a pond behind it. This gives the beaver safe access to even more trees.

Last night for dinner—guess what?—the beaver ate . . .

A Life in the Water

Beavers' bodies are perfectly adapted for the life they lead. Their ears and noses have valves that close up when they are underwater. Their eyes have thin films that cover and protect them from the water. But the film allows the beavers to see where they are going. Even their lips help them out. They seal tightly behind two big front teeth. That way, a beaver's mouth doesn't fill with water while he's tugging a birch branch through the creek.

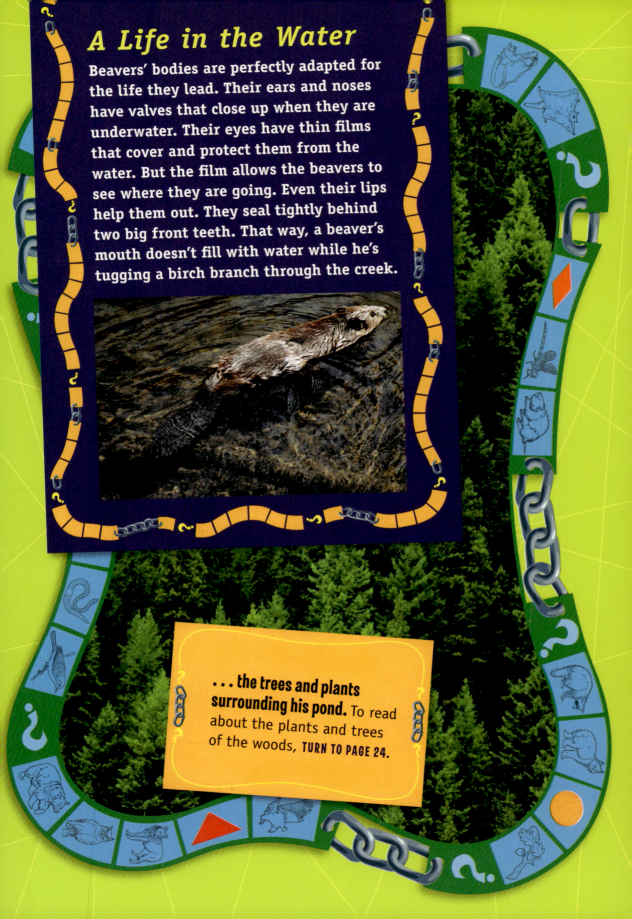

. . . **the trees and plants surrounding his pond.** To read about the plants and trees of the woods, **TURN TO PAGE 24.**

INSECTS

The woods buzz with insects in the warm weather. Bees zoom, horseflies nip, gnats hatch, moths flutter, ants march, and mosquitoes hum. These insects are a crucial part of the food chain of the forest. Many creatures survive just by eating insects alone. And the work insects do in the forest helps other creatures' lives.

Still, not all insects benefit forest life. Sometimes people or animals bring in insects that aren't naturally found in the forest. These new species don't have any natural predators. And the existing species don't have any defenses against the invaders. The new insects often quickly overcome the native ones. This can spell disaster for the forest.

emerald ash borer

carpenter ants

Currently, scientists have their eyes on two invading beetles—the emerald ash borer and the Asian longhorned beetle. These beetles have the potential to attack and kill millions of ash and maple trees. But there's still not much scientists can do except watch and wait.

Most insects in the woods are primary consumers. They live off the plants and trees of the woods.

To read about the plants and trees of the woods, **TURN TO PAGE 24.**

monarch butterfly

A swarm of insects passes through a shaft of light in the forest.

BALD EAGLE *(Haliaeetus leucocephalus)*

The bald eagle pumps her wings, soaring higher and higher over the lake. She scans the waters and the shoreline, looking for **prey.** From up here, she can see for nearly 3 miles (5 kilometers) around. And she sees incredible detail, such as that squirrel scurrying along the shore almost a mile (1.6 km) away. The eagle's eyes can see straight ahead and to the side at the same time. Her excellent vision helps her to hunt for food. And she is always looking. Back home in her nest, she has two hungry eaglets that depend on her and her mate for their meals.

Down below, she spies the shadow of a fish near the surface of the water. The eagle tucks back her wings and dives sharply. She hits the water at 100 miles (160 km) per hour. Splash! Her talons stretch out. She snatches the fish.

A bald eagle snatches a fish from a forest lake.

DDT

Not too long ago, this bald eagle would have led you to a dead end of the food web. Bald eagles were declared an endangered species in 1967. There were fewer than 450 pairs left in the United States. Part of the bald eagles' problem was caused by people using a pesticide, or insect poison, called DDT. DDT was sprayed over ponds, fields, and even cities to kill insects such as mosquitoes. But the DDT was poisonous for many animals. It caused eagles' eggshells to be extremely thin. The shells often broke before the eaglets were ready to hatch, and the eaglets died.

The use of DDT was banned in the United States in the 1970s. The government also took other steps to protect the bald eagle, such as making it illegal to hunt them. Bald eagles in the wild have since made an amazing comeback. In June 2007, wildlife officials removed the bald eagle from the endangered species list. But some people think the eagle should continue to be protected. What do you think?

But wait! The fish fights back. And this fish is stronger and heavier than she expected. The eagle starts to sink into the water.

The eagle isn't about to give up this fish, though. She pulls her wings through the water like oars and starts to swim the short distance to the shore. Once there, she drags the fish up on land. She dries her wings and takes off for home, the fish clutched in her talons.

Home is an enormous nest, or aerie, at the top of a white pine tree. The aerie is huge, about the size of a small bedroom. It buzzes with flies from the rotten, stinky leftovers of the eagle's last meal left at the bottom of the nest.

A bald eagle feeds one of its eaglets.

The eagle shreds a piece of fish for the two hungry eaglets. She gulps down bits of fish for herself too. It doesn't matter if she swallows scales or bones. She has a special pouch near her stomach that collects the things she can't digest. Later, she'll spit them back up. She might throw up bits from her earlier meals too. *Last night for dinner, the eagle feasted on . . .*

. . . a Kirtland's warbler out collecting bits for her nest. To see what another Kirtland's warbler is up to, TURN TO PAGE 15.

. . . a northern short-tailed shrew trying to scurry across a field unnoticed. To see what another northern short-tailed shrew is up to, TURN TO PAGE 54.

. . . a northern pike pulled from water. To see what another northern pike is up to, TURN TO PAGE 58.

. . . a bullfrog grabbed in midleap from a lily pad. To see what another bullfrog is up to, TURN TO PAGE 16.

. . . a northern ringneck snake basking in the warm sun on a log. To see what another northern ringneck snake is up to, TURN TO PAGE 42.

. . . the body of a white-tailed deer at the side of the highway. To see what another white-tailed deer is up to, TURN TO PAGE 46.

. . . a muskrat gliding through the shallow water. To see what another muskrat is up to, TURN TO PAGE 12.

. . . a Canada goose gosling that strayed too far from his mother. To see what another Canada goose is up to, TURN TO PAGE 52.

NORTHERN RINGNECK SNAKE

(Diadophis punctatus edwardsi)

The northern ringneck snake hides under the leaves at the edge of the log, watching and waiting for food to pass by. Northern ringneck snakes are not rare, but they are very rarely seen. They like to hide under the layer of dead leaves, or in logs or stumps.

Suddenly, the wind shifts, and the leaves the snake was hiding under are blown away. Look out! He is out in the open. And something is watching him. Is it an owl? A shrew?

Immediately, the snake rolls and twists, showing off his yellow underbelly as a warning. Then a strong scent floats through the air. It is a liquid released by the snake—another warning to leave it alone. But even though he looks and smells scary, a northern ringneck rarely bites to defend himself.

The danger passes. Then the snake sees a creature in front of him. It's a young mouse. And she's just the right size for a meal. The snake makes a grab for the mouse. He wraps himself around her, squeezing tighter and tighter, until she can't breath. Then he begins the slow process of swallowing her whole.

The snake has been lucky lately. A predator could have caught a glimpse of him just as easily. Instead, this marks the second night in a row that the snake has been well fed. *Last night for dinner he had . . .*

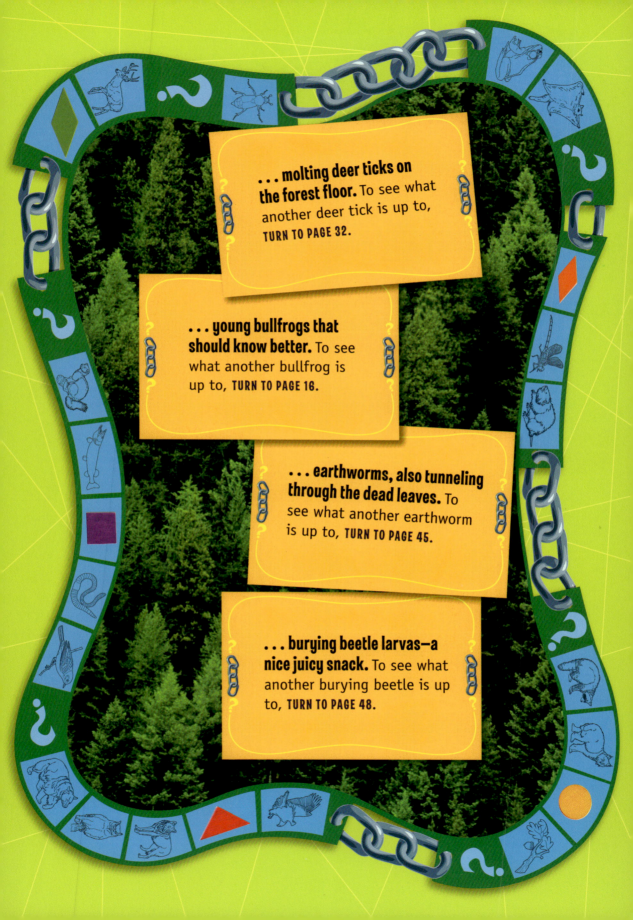

. . . **molting deer ticks on the forest floor.** To see what another deer tick is up to, TURN TO PAGE 32.

. . . **young bullfrogs that should know better.** To see what another bullfrog is up to, TURN TO PAGE 16.

. . . **earthworms, also tunneling through the dead leaves.** To see what another earthworm is up to, TURN TO PAGE 45.

. . . **burying beetle larvas—a nice juicy snack.** To see what another burying beetle is up to, TURN TO PAGE 48.

A FOREST FOOD WEB

In the forest, energy moves around the food chain from the sun to plants, from plants to plant eaters, and from animals to the creatures that eat them.

44

EARTHWORMS *(Lumbricus terrestris)*

An earthworm tunnels through the dirt on the forest floor. It stretches and then contracts (pulls in) its strong muscles to move. Each segment of the worm has invisible bristles that pull it along. As the worm plows through the dirt, it loosens the soil to let in water and air. This makes it easier for the roots of the woodland plants to reach down and grow.

Earthworms are also decomposers. As the worm moves, it mixes the nutrients from the dead leaves on the surface further into the ground. The earthworm also digests the **bacteria** and **decomposing** material. The juices in its stomach break down its food. Then the earthworm releases the digested food as poop. This poop helps the soil too.

While worms do help some plants to grow, they're hurting others. Earthworms are actually an invasive species to North America. That means that they aren't found here naturally. European settlers brought them over a few centuries ago on ships and wagon wheels.

Earthworms spread quickly—they can double their population in just a few months. Now worms are found nearly everywhere in North America. As the worms move to more North American forests, they eat up the dead leaf material on the ground. This keeps the forest floors clear of a thick carpet of leaves and decaying plants. Many plants' seeds can grow only in that leafy material. So some plant species are becoming **extinct**—all because of earthworms.

45

To read about the plants and trees of the woods, TURN TO PAGE 24

WHITE-TAILED DEER *(Odocoileus virginianus)*

The white-tailed deer yanks up the grass under a tree. He swallows it whole. Later on, he'll spit it back up as cud—food mixed with stomach juices. The deer chews the cud and reswallows it. Like cows, deer are **ruminants**—they have four parts to their stomachs. In the first two stomachs, food mixes with bile, a fluid that helps break down the food. The food and bile make cud. After the deer reswallows his cud, it goes to the third stomach and then to the fourth to be further digested.

Unlike other forest animals, deer are growing in number. Farmland gives them even more opportunity to graze. Meanwhile, their traditional predators—wolves and large cats—have become scarce. But there is a limit to how many deer the land can support. There have been instances where deer have starved to death because there was not enough food for the herd.

Large numbers of deer cause other problems too. They get into people's gardens and do a lot of damage. They spread tick-borne diseases such as Lyme disease. And they wander onto roads and highways where they get hit by automobiles or cause accidents. Most places in North America allow people to hunt deer to help control the deer population. The deer hunters do a job once done by the large carnivores of the forest.

There are not many choices for meals for deer. They are **herbivores** and live off the plants, bushes, and trees of the forest.

To read about the plants and trees of the woods, TURN TO PAGE 24

Bucks' Antlers

Bucks, or male deer, shed and regrow their antlers every year. As the antlers grow through the spring and summer, they are fed by a supply of blood. During this time, the antlers have rounded tips and are covered in a soft fuzz called velvet. In the fall, the blood supply to the antlers is cut off. Then the bucks rub their antlers on anything they can find. The velvet comes off, and the antlers look hard and smooth, almost like bone. The tips are no longer rounded—they come to a point. By the next spring, they fall off and new ones are ready to grow.

And, in case you were wondering, you can't tell how old a deer is by the number of points on his antler. Instead, scientists look at a deer's teeth to guess the animal's age.

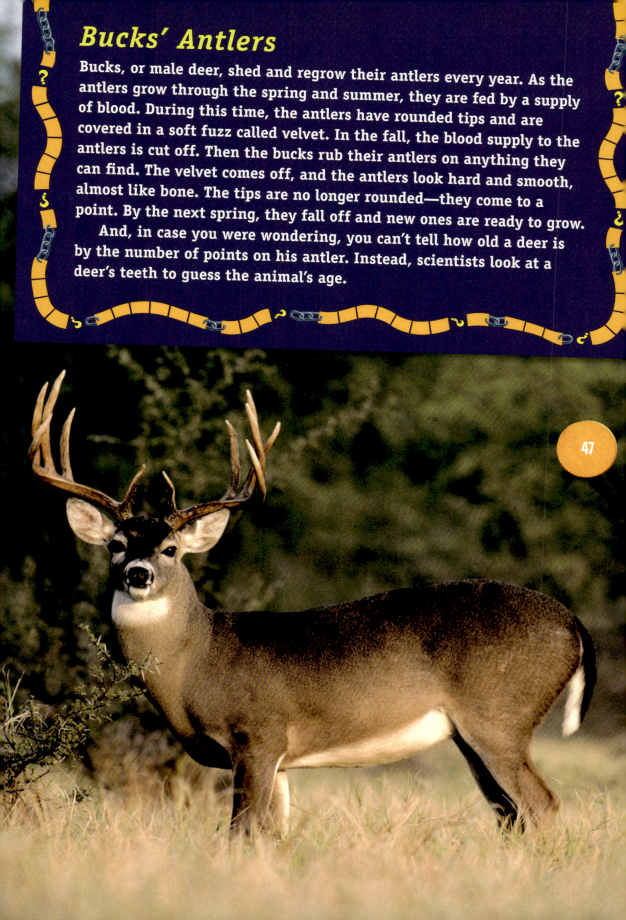

BURYING BEETLES *(Nicrophorus sayi)*

Burying beetles bury the dead of the forest. When an animal dies in the forest, these decomposers are there within hours.

A male and female pair sniff out a dead mouse from almost 2 miles (3 kilometers) away. They buzz across the woods and drop down near the body. Slowly, they tug the body to a soft area. Beetles move the body by lying on their backs and shifting it with their feet. When they get it where they want, they start digging under the body. Eventually, the mouse falls in the hole and is buried.

Now they go to work underground. The beetles pull off small bits of flesh and wrap it in their juices to save for their **larvas**. Their larvas are laid in the ground next to the body. One of the most unusual things about these beetles is that they care for their young. Most insects don't. These beetles will feed their babies bits of food until they're big enough to live on their own.

Despite the big job they do in the forest, some burying beetles—such as the American burying beetle—are becoming rarer and are in danger of becoming **extinct**. Scientists think it's simply because there are fewer animals in the woods, so there are fewer animals' bodies for burying beetles to eat.

Fortunately, that is not the case for this little family. *Last night they had their choice of meals...*

. . . a dead bullfrog. To see what another bullfrog is up to, TURN TO PAGE 16.

. . . a dead Kirtland's warbler. To see what another Kirtland's warbler is up to, TURN TO PAGE 15.

. . . a dead northern short-tailed shrew. To see what another northern short-tailed shrew is up to, TURN TO PAGE 54.

. . . a dead northern flying squirrel. To see what another northern flying squirrel is up to, TURN TO PAGE 19.

RACCOON *(Procyon lotor)*

The raccoon dips the berries in the water at the edge of the lake. Her front paws, which look very much like human hands, turn and pat the fruit. Her scientific name, *lotor,* means "one who washes." But the raccoon isn't really washing her food before she eats it. Her paws have thousands of nerve endings. Touching and feeling her food is one way she learns about it.

Raccoons are very intelligent. They are smarter than cats and white rats and just slightly less intelligent than monkeys. Their brainpower is almost certainly part of the reason the raccoon has adapted so well to living among humans. In fact, more raccoons now live in cities and suburbs than in the woods!

This raccoon gobbles down the berries and makes her way back to her den in a tree hollow. Her babies wait there. Like all raccoons, they were born deaf and blind, with black skin and yellowish fur. When they get bigger, their mother will take them out of the den. She'll carry them by the back of their necks, just as a cat carries kittens. But for now, they just need her milk. And to supply it, she needs to keep eating.

Luckily, raccoons will eat just about anything. That's another reason they do so well in many environments. ***Last night for dinner, this raccoon chewed on . . .***

A raccoon learns about its food by feeling it and dipping it in water.

. . . the tiny eggs of the **Kirtland's warbler.** To see what another Kirtland's warbler is up to, TURN TO PAGE 15.

. . . **a young bullfrog leaping along the shore.** To see what another bullfrog is up to, TURN TO PAGE 16.

. . . **a deer tick that fell out of the raccoon's own fur.** To see what another deer tick is up to, TURN TO PAGE 32.

. . . **a northern ringneck snake.** To see what another northern ringneck snake is up to, TURN TO PAGE 42.

. . . **the remains of a muskrat caught in a trap.** To see what another muskrat is up to, TURN TO PAGE 12.

. . . **Canada goose eggs hidden in the tall grass.** To see what another Canada goose is up to, TURN TO PAGE 52.

. . . **two burying beetles found by scratching in the dirt.** To see what another burying beetle is up to, TURN TO PAGE 48.

. . . **more nuts and berries from the trees.** To read about the plants and trees of the woods, TURN TO PAGE 24.

CANADA GOOSE
(B. canadensis maxima)

Honk! The flying goose skids across the surface of the lake in northern Wisconsin. He is part of the Mississippi Valley Population, a group of more than one million geese. Each fall and spring, the Mississippi Valley Population flies between the southern United States and Canada along the Mississippi River. The group will stop and stay a few weeks in this wetland to rest. Canada geese were almost extinct one hundred years ago, but their numbers became strong again.

Some geese do not migrate, or fly to another region, in winter anymore. Most animals migrate to warmer climates to look for food. But Canada geese live throughout the year in cities and suburbs. They gather near parks and ponds, eat all the grass, and leave their poop behind.

People try to figure out why the geese aren't migrating. Longer periods of warm weather might be one reason. And handouts from people provide the geese with year-round food. But there are no handouts out here in the forest. The goose must look hard for food. *Last night for dinner, he found . . .*

Flying in Formation

Why do geese fly in a V formation? Flying in diagonal lines, one behind one another, helps the geese to lessen the air that is pushing against them when they fly. They can fly faster and for longer distances before they get tired. So what about the leader—the point of the V? Well, when he (or she) gets tired, he simply drifts back to the end of the line. There he can enjoy the easier flight and rest up. Eventually, all the birds in a V take a turn leading. Scientists aren't sure how the geese all know where they are going, though.

. . . a blood-filled deer tick on the ground. To see what another deer tick is up to, TURN TO PAGE 32.

. . . a Hine's emerald dragonfly clinging to the marsh grass. To see what another Hine's emerald dragonfly is up to, TURN TO PAGE 23.

. . . insects. Grass and grains are a goose's preferred food. But a goose is not above snatching a bug or two for a snack. To read about other insects of the woods, TURN TO PAGE 36.

. . . grass and plants near the water—a lot of them! Geese have to eat almost a half a pound (0.2 kilograms) of food a day. To read about the plants and trees of the woods, TURN TO PAGE 24.

NORTHERN SHORT-TAILED SHREW

(Blarina brevicauda)

The northern short-tailed shrew scuttles across the forest floor. She moves through a shallow tunnel she's created just under the leaves. It keeps her hidden from bigger animals looking for a snack.

But the shrew doesn't depend on her eyes to find her way back to her nest. Her eyes can only tell her if it's light or dark. Shrews don't see shapes at all. Instead, she finds her way by feeling things out with her sensitive whiskers. She also sends out a high-pitched sound. The sound's echo comes bouncing back to her. From that echo, she can tell the size and location of things in her path—such as the cozy nest that she's just entered.

Like most shrews, she's created a large nest, almost 8 inches (20 centimeters) across. It has several exits, just in case she needs to make a quick escape. It's almost like a shrew-sized apartment. She uses the different rooms for different things. One is a sleeping room. Another is used as a bathroom (but no flushing toilet!). Yet another is her kitchen. She stores her food there, such as her dinner from last night. ***Tonight on her kitchen floor she finds . . .***

Poison!

The northern short-tailed shrew is the only mammal in North America that uses venom, a poison used on **prey**. Her salivary gland, a small organ in the throat, produces the venom. When the shrew bites her prey, the venom shoots through a groove in her teeth. The poison paralyzes her prey, making them unable to move or escape. Her poisonous teeth allow the shrew to feast on prey bigger than what an animal her size would normally be able to catch. The animals and insects bitten by a shrew can remain alive but paralyzed for days. This gives the shrew fresh food to feast on.

. . . a Kirtland's warbler that was out in search of seeds. To see what another Kirtland's warbler is up to, TURN TO PAGE 15.

. . . a Hine's emerald dragonfly that she pounced on while he was drying his wings. To see what another Hine's emerald dragonfly is up to, TURN TO PAGE 23.

. . . another northern short-tailed shrew!

. . . a bullfrog that hopped by one of her tunnels. To see what another bullfrog is up to, TURN TO PAGE 16.

. . . a small northern ringneck snake that was too curious about one of the shrew's entrance holes. To see what another northern ringneck snake is up to, TURN TO PAGE 42.

. . . a burying beetle that crossed her path. To see what another burying beetle is up to, TURN TO PAGE 48.

. . . insects that the shrew found flitting on a stump nearby. To read about insects of the woods, TURN TO PAGE 36.

. . . a stash of seeds she collected from nearby plants. To learn about plants and trees of the woods, TURN TO PAGE 24.

PINE MARTEN *(Martes americana)*

The pine marten streaks across the forest floor after a red squirrel. The marten is similar in size and shape to a weasel. But she has soft, glossy fur and a bushy tail. The marten nabs the squirrel, killing it quickly with a bite to the back of its neck.

While they are not officially endangered in the United States or Canada, martens are on many regional **endangered species lists**. Scientists guess that once there was one marten in every square mile (1.6 square kilometers) of forest. But martens began to disappear in the early 1900s. This happened about the same time that most of the trees in the woods were cut down for lumber. Suddenly, the martens had nowhere to live. In addition to a loss of habitat, martens also suffered from human hunters. People trapped martens for their reddish brown fur. This marten is one of the few left.

Some local governments are trying to reintroduce, or bring back, the martens to the woods. But the martens are not spreading very quickly. We have learned that martens aren't happy in just any group of trees. They need the thick **canopies** and fallen logs of old forests. And old forests take time to grow— more than one hundred years.

Hopefully, this pine marten and her babies can hang on and wait. But right now, she's more concerned with day-to-day survival. ***Last night for dinner, she tracked down . . .***

. . . a northern short-tailed shrew, but it doesn't taste very good. To see what another northern short-tailed shrew is up to, TURN TO PAGE 54.

. . . a northern flying squirrel—the marten's favorite meal. To see what another northern flying squirrel is up to, TURN TO PAGE 19.

. . . nuts and berries from nearby trees. To read about the plants and trees of the woods, TURN TO PAGE 24.

. . . insects such as beetles and moths. To read about the other insects of the woods, TURN TO PAGE 36.

NORTHERN PIKE (Esox lucius)

The northern pike lies still in the thick tangle of underwater weeds. His body curves in an S shape. He might look like he's resting, but he's just waiting for his next meal.

The pike sees in almost every direction. He watches a long, dark shadow sweep by. It's a muskellunge (or musky), a fish almost as long as an eight-year-old human is tall. Northern pikes can grow that big too, but this one is still young. He stays hidden so he doesn't end up as a meal for the musky.

Ah, something flashes! With a twitch of his tail and fins, the pike lunges. His victim doesn't have a chance. The pike hits fast, in a fraction of a second. His strong needlelike teeth slant backward for a good grip on his **prey**. *Locked in the pike's jaws is . . .*

Shrinking Pikes

Northern pikes are getting smaller. Scientists think it's because people are catching too many of the big ones. They also think it's because some lakes' deep waters have less oxygen in them because of increasing amounts of algae. Too much algae means more algae-eating bacteria. And the increase in bacteria uses up the oxygen. As pikes grow, they have to move out to cooler, deeper water to feed. There's usually more oxygen in deeper water. But if the deeper water is no better, the pikes don't eat as much. And they don't grow as big.

. . . **a wiggling Hine's emerald dragonfly nymph.** Crunch. To see what another Hine's emerald dragonfly is up to, TURN TO PAGE 23.

. . . **a bullfrog under a lily pad.** To see what another bullfrog is up to, TURN TO PAGE 16.

. . . **a northern short-tailed shrew getting a sip of water.** To see what another northern short-tailed shrew is up to, TURN TO PAGE 54.

. . . **a young American beaver swimming across the bay.** To see what another American beaver is up to, TURN TO PAGE 34.

. . . **a Canada goose gosling that's paddled a little too far away from her mother.** To see what another Canada goose is up to, TURN TO PAGE 52.

GLOSSARY

bacteria: tiny living things made up of only one cell

canopy: the highest branchy layer of a forest. It is formed by the treetops.

carnivore: an animal that eats other animals

decomposers: living things, such as insects or bacteria, that feed on dead plants and animals

decomposing: decaying, or breaking down, after dying

endangered species list: a list of animals that are in danger of becoming extinct

extinct: no longer existing

food chain: a system in which energy moves from the sun to plants and to animals as each eats and is eaten

food web: many food chains linked together

habitats: areas where a plant or animal naturally lives and grows

herbivores: an animal that eats plants

larva: the wormlike stage in an insect's life between the egg and adult forms

mammals: animals that have hair and feed their babies milk from their bodies

nutrients: substances, especially in food, that help a plant or animal survive

nymph: a young insect almost at the adult stage

omnivores: animals that eat meat and plants

parasites: organisms that live on or with a living plant or animal and use it to get food

predators: animals that hunt and kill other animals for food

prey: animals that are hunted for food by other animals

primary consumers: animals that eat plants

producers: living things, such as plants, that make their own food

ruminants: hoofed animals that have multichambered stomachs for breaking down hard-to-digest food

secondary consumers: animals and insects that eat other animals and insects

species: a group of related animals or plants

tertiary consumers: animals that eat other animals and that have few natural enemies

FURTHER READING AND WEBSITES

Butterfield, Moira. *Protecting Temperate Forests*. Milwaukee: Gareth Stevens, 2005. Butterfield examines the issues and problems facing temperate forests.

Dendy, Leslie A. *Tracks, Scats and Signs*. Minnetonka, MN: NorthWord, 1996. This Take-Along guide includes fun activities and projects to help readers learn how to identify animals in the wild.

Environmental Education for Kids (EEK!)
http://www.dnr.state.wi.us/eek
This Wisconsin Department of Natural Resources website is dedicated to educating kids about temperate forest wildlife and habitats.

Macmillan, Dianne M. *Life in a Deciduous Forest*. Minneapolis: Twenty-First Century Books, 2003. This book looks at the features, processes, and species that make up the ecosystem of a deciduous forest.

Markle, Sandra. *Wolves*. Minneapolis: Lerner Publications Company, 2004. This book, part of the Animal Predators series, shows the hunting habits and group behavior of gray wolves.

Nadeau, Isaac. *Food Chains in a Forest Habitat*. New York: PowerKids Press, 2002. Learn more about the relationships and interactions among forest creatures.

Peterson First Guides. New York: Houghton Mifflin. This series is a young reader's version of the Peterson Field Guides. Each book covers an aspect of North American nature and wildlife—insects, birds, trees, reptiles, amphibians, and many more.

U.S. Fish and Wildlife Service Kids' Corner
http://www.fws.gov/endangered/kids/index.html
Find out about the United States' Endangered Species Act and what can be done to help the animals on the endangered and threatened lists.

SELECTED BIBLIOGRAPHY

Hartley, H. T. Jackson. *Mammals of Wisconsin*. Madison: University of Wisconsin Press, 1961.

Hinterland's Who's Who. 2008. http://www.hww.ca (February 20, 2008).

Kurta, Allen. *Mammals of the Great Lakes Region*. Ann Arbor: University of Michigan Press, 1995.

Michigan Department of Natural Resources. 2008. http://www.michigan.gov/dnr (February 20, 2008).

National Audubon Society Field Guides Series. New York: Alfred A. Knopf, 1994–2002.

University of Michigan Museum of Zoology. *Animal Diversity Web*. 1995–2008. http://animaldiversity.ummz.umich.edu (February 20, 2008).

U.S. Fish and Wildlife Service. 2008. http://www.fws.gov (February 20, 2008).

Vogt, Richard Carl. *Natural History of Amphibians and Reptiles of Wisconsin*. Milwaukee: Milwaukee Public Museum and Friends of the Museum, 1981.

Wisconsin Department of Natural Resources. "Animals, Plants, and Natural Communities." 2007. http://dnr.wi.gov/org/land/er/biodiversity.htm (February 20, 2008).

INDEX

American beaver (*Castor canadensis*), 34

American black bear (*Ursus americanus*), 8–10

Asian longhorned beetle, 36

babies, 8–10, 15, 23, 28, 38, 40, 48, 50, 56

bald eagle (*Haliaeetus leucocephalus*), 38–40

bullfrog (*Rana catesbeiana* Shaw), 16–17

burying beetles (*Nicrophorus sayi*), 48

Canada goose (*B. canadensis maxima*), 52

Canada lynx (*Lynx canadensis*), 27

climate of temperate forest, 5

consumers, definitions of: primary consumer, 6; secondary consumer, 6; tertiary consumer, 6

decomposers, 6, 45, 48

deer tick (*Ixodes scapularis*), 32, 46

earthworm (*Lumbricus terrestris*), 45

elk (*Cervus elaphus*), 14, 29

emerald ash borer, 36

endangered species, 14, 15, 23, 27, 39, 48, 52, 56

fish, 10, 38, 40, 58

gray wolf (*Canis lupus*), 28–30

great horned owl (*Bubo virginianus*), 20–21, 42

ground layer of forest, 25

herb layer of forest, 24

Hine's emerald dragonfly (*Somatochlora hineana*), 23

humans, 21, 32, 46, 50, 52; and deforestation, 4, 14, 56; and hunting, 10, 12, 14, 29–30, 58; other negative effects of, 9, 15, 19, 23, 27, 36, 45; and pesticides, 23, 39; positive effects of, 29, 56

insects, 4, 36–37, 48

Kirtland's warbler (*Dendroica kirtlandii*), 15

mosquito, 23, 36

muskrat (*Ondatra zibethicus*), 12

nests, 15, 21, 40

northern flying squirrel (*Glaucomys sabrinus*), 19

northern pike (*Esox lucius*), 58

northern ringneck snake (*Diadophis punctatus edwardsi*), 42

northern short-tailed shrew (*Blarina brevicauda*), 54, 42

parasite, 15, 17, 32

photosynthesis (diagram), 24

pine marten (*Martes americana*), 56

plants, 4, 6, 24–25, 45, 46

producers, 6, 24–25

raccoon (*Procyon lotor*), 50

temperate forest, 4

trees, 4, 9, 15, 19, 20, 24–25, 34; canopy, 24, 56

water, 24–25, 40, 50; as habitat, 12, 16, 23, 34–35, 52, 58

white-tailed deer (*Odocoileus virginianus*), 4

Photo Acknowledgments

The images in this book are used with the permission of: © David R. Frazier/ Stone/Getty Images, pp. 1, 4-5, 6-7, 11, 13, 18, 22, 26, 31, 33, 35, 41, 43, 49, 51, 53, 55, 57, 59; © Konrad Wothe/Minden Pictures/Getty Images, pp. 8, 29; © age fotostock/SuperStock, pp. 9, 12, 14, 36 (top); © Riccardo Savi/Stone/ Getty Images, p. 10; © William Leaman/Alamy, p. 15 (top); © Ross Frid/Visuals Unlimited, p. 15 (bottom); © David Northcott/Danita Delimont/Alamy, p. 16; © Gary Meszaros/Photo Researchers, Inc., p. 17; © Richard Alan Wood/ Animals Animals, p. 19; © Michael Durham/Minden Pictures/Getty Images, p. 20; © Photodisc/Getty Images, pp. 21 (top), 34, 35, 36 (bottom), 38, 39, 47; © Rich Kirchner/NHPA/Photoshot, p. 21 (bottom); © Paul Burton, p. 23; © Paul Edmondson/Photodisc/Getty Images, p. 24 (top); © Bill Hauser/Independent Picture Service, p. 24 (bottom); © Gay Bumgarner/Photographer's Choice/Getty Images, p. 25 (top left); © Steve Maslowski/Visuals Unlimited, pp. 25 (top right), 42, 45; © Ned Therrien/Visuals Unlimited, p. 25 (bottom); © iStockphoto .com/Carolina K. Smith, M.D., p. 27; © Jim & Jamie Dutcher/National Geographic/Getty Images, pp. 28, 30; © Dr. James Castner/Visuals Unlimited, p. 32; © Kim Taylor/Dorling Kindersley/Getty Images, p. 36 (center); © Lee Rentz/Bruce Coleman, Inc., p. 37; © Roy Toft/National Geographic/Getty Images, p. 40; © Purestock/Getty Images, p. 46; © Altrendo Nature/Getty Images, p. 48; © Cheryl Ertelt/Visuals Unlimited, p. 50; © Thomas Kitchin & Victoria Hurst/All Canada Photos/Getty Images, p. 52 (top); © Burazin/ Photographer's Choice/Getty Images, p. 52 (bottom); © Rob and Ann Simpson/ Visuals Unlimited, p. 54; U.S. Fish and Wildlife Service, p. 56; © Wil Meinderts/ Foto Natura/Minden Pictures/Getty Images, p. 58. Illustrations for game board and pieces © Bill Hauser/Independent Picture Service.

Front Cover: © David R. Frazier/Stone/Getty Images (background); © iStockphoto.com/David Hutchison (left); U.S. Fish and Wildlife Service (second from left); © Todd Strand/Independent Picture Service (second from right); © Gary Meszaros/Visuals Unlimited (right).

About the Authors

Don and Becky Wojahn are school library media specialists by day and writers by night. Their natural habitat is the temperate forests of northwestern Wisconsin, where they share their den with two animal-loving sons and two big black dogs. The Wojahns' other Follow that Food Chain books include *A Desert Food Chain*, *A Rain Forest Food Chain*, *A Savanna Food Chain*, *A Tundra Food Chain*, and *An Australian Outback Food Chain*.